Structured Analysis Primer
for
CAPAs & Process Improvement

The How of 6 Sigma

By

J. J. Haefner

Introduction

So many years ago on the first day of my new job as a process engineer, my supervisor Dick Bomball welcomed me into his group of engineers and gave me the 3.5 x 6 inch laminated card below. The Participative Problem Solving Skills, G.I.S.T., became my guide henceforth.

PARTICIPATIVE PROBLEM SOLVING SKILLS (G-I-S-T)

G - GATHERING INFORMATION
    1. Greeting
    2. General question.
    3. Second general question.
    4. Six Q's.
       a. What
       b. Where
       c. When
       d. Who
       e. Why
       f. Extent or degree
    5. Cause Identification Check List (CICL)
       a. Could people be a part of the problem?
       b. " system or procedure be part of problem?
       c. " working conditions   "   "   "   "   ?
       d. " equipment or material "   "   "   "   ?
       e. " communications   "   "   "   "   ?
    6. What has changed?

I - IDENTIFY THE PROBLEM IN TERMS OF
    1. Symptoms   - What actually is happening.
    2. Obstacles - Why is it different.
    3. Goals   - What should be happening.

S - SEEK SOLUTIONS
    1. State limits on solutions in terms of:
       a. People.
       b. Money.
       c. Time.
    2. Give employes a chance to suggest solutions.
    3. Evaluate and eliminate solutions by answering:
       a. How will that solution help?
       b. What won't it do?
       c. What other problems could it cause?
    4. Obtain multiple alternatives.

T - TAKING ACTION
    1. Choose an acceptable solution.
    2. State a plan of action which includes:
       a. What will be done?
       b. Who will do it?
       c. When it will be done?
    3. Verify understanding of action plan.
    4. Close discussion.
    5. Critique discussion.

Participative Problem Solving

The four major steps in G.I.S.T. were:

- o Gather information: what, where, when, who, why, scope.
- o Identify the problem in terms of people, environment, machine, material, and communications.
- o Seek solutions.
- o Take actions.

On the back of the card was a matrix to help narrow the scope and focus of the project.

	WHAT	WHERE	WHEN	WHO	WHY	EXTENT
PEOPLE						
SYSTEM/ PROCEDURE						
CONDITIONS						
EQUIPMENT/ MATERIAL						
COMMUNICATIONS						

Is/Is Not Scope Matrix

Participated problem solving is cited as a 1973 General Motors program. It preceded Quality Circles and even Kaoru Ishikawa's

1982 Guide to Quality Control that became a popular early standard that introduced the 7 Quality Tools. GIST had similar quality tools including the fishbone diagram elements, graphs, is/is not, worker input, team collaboration, and a structured method for attacking and resolving problems. I took my GIST card, a new personal computer to which I added Statgraphics statistical software, and began my career as a process/quality engineer. Within a few months, I was solving production problems that had remained unresolved for years and eliminated millions of dollars of scrap along the way.

Forward to 2015 where, as a consulting engineer and statistician in the medical manufacturing, I have encountered Ph. d. statisticians, 6 Sigma Black Belts, and numerous quality engineers who understood 6 Sigma's define, measure, analyze, improve, and control (DMAIC) very well but did not understand how to efficiently solve the problems at hand. A review of the PowerPoint training materials from prominent 6 Sigma consulting groups and organizations suggests a lack of a discrete *structure* for conducting an improvement project. A discrete structure, in addition to the statistics and engineering methods training, fills a void in methodology that can only enhance the prospect for project success.

This structured analysis primer has its roots in G.I.S.T and, presumably, was derived from the 1950's Kepner-Tregoe methods, and some Japanese pre-quality circle activities from the 1960s. It is enhanced by the subsequent refinement of numerous process analysis methods: 6/7/8-D, 7 Step, 5 Ys, 14 Step, and more. This primer has been the guide for hundreds of projects and was the main vehicle for process analysis and improvement that led to Credit Union National Association (CUNA) winning the predecessor to the Wisconsin Forward Award by improving one CUNA division in every category of the Malcolm-Baldrige Award. One CUNA team used Structured Analysis to complete a credit union improvement that helped credit unions nation-wide and subsequently won the RIT/USA Today Quality Crystal in 1993.

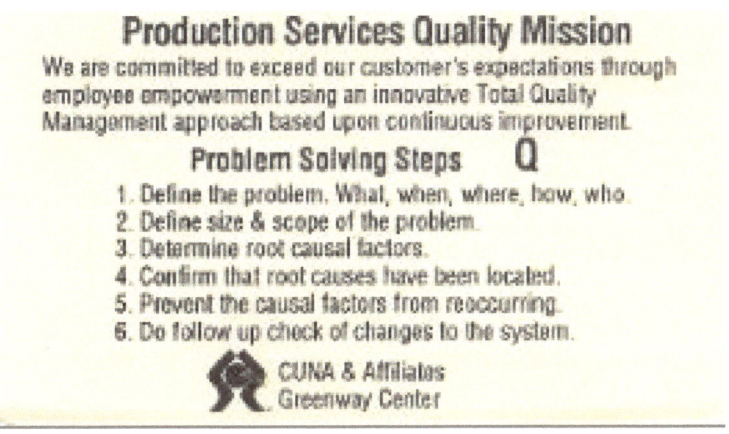

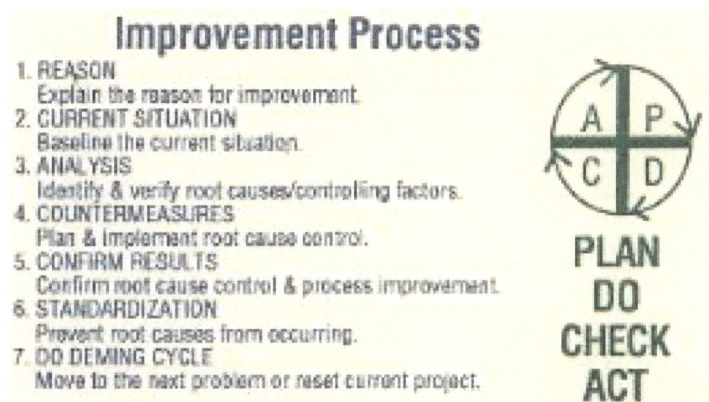

CUNA CSG Cards

Structured Analysis

Phase 1: Determine the Project Focus or Theme (Check/Define-Global Measure)

1.1 Select the project

1.1.1. Identify general issues. The most likely sources for projects are customer complaints, internal scrap, or insufficient product feature capability. In this step, simply state one of them or whatever other compelling situation is prompting the project. Opportunities may also come from customer input, worker suggestions, manager feedback, corporate strategic directives, or simple databases of data.

Organizational problems are also an excellent source for improvement projects. Non-competitive products, low service volumes, high product or service cost, not focusing on the vital few customers or repeated service failures are typical improvement project material.

The output from this task can be a specific problem or a list of improvement opportunities.

1.1.2. Understand the issue from the customers perspective. In this step customers and how they may be affected by the issue are identified. Customer needs or requirements are cited.

This step results in a measurable understanding of how customers are affected. This is a good time to quantify customer perspective in dollars.

1.1.3. Describe the procedure used and develop boundaries.
Determine the project boundaries. The question must be answered "at what point in the process do our studies begin?" And, "At what point in the process do we not go beyond in our studies of the process?"

1.1.4. Determine the theme or goal and identify the measure(s) of progress.
The theme has a direction, a process, and a measure. Sample themes could be: to reduce the amount of time to complete a credit card application." In this example, the direction is *reduce*. The measure is *time*. The process is *credit card application*. Another project might be: to improve the oxygen sensor accuracy of a perfusion machine.

When all of the components of step 1.1 are completed then the team can move to step 1.2.

2.1 Charter stating the reason(s) for and the value of the project

Step 2.1 explains why this project is important and provides information about the team: participants, job functions, department, and so on. This can be a project statement and is often similar to a 6 Sigma Charter that includes a team name,

5.1.1. Implement the improvements on a small scale ("Do"). The objective of this task is to test the effectiveness of the proposed improvement(s). This is the pilot phase. Regardless of all of the best planning and analysis, sometimes the proposed improvements do not yield the intended results. This is why small-scale implementation is important.

This task also prepares the organization for the full-scale implementation by specifying the five W's and two H's of the implementation:

- Who is going to make the small-scale improvements?
- What is going to be improved?
- Where will the improvements be made?
- When will the improvements be made?
- Why are the improvements being made?
- How will the improvements be made?
- How much are the improvements going to cost?

5.1.2. Study the small-scale implementation ("Check"). The results of the small-scale implementation determine whether the full-scale implementation will be conducted. The key here is to check the baseline data to see if the improvements have the desired results. To do this, you ask the question, Have the root causes or controlling factors of the process been adequately affected?

a theme, operational definitions, a list of team members, the team leader, the facilitator, measure(s) of progress, key support people, possible sponsor, meeting information, project boundaries, barriers, aids, and meeting ground rules.

Project Charter

Project Name:	
Business Case:	

Problem/Opportunity:	Scope, Constraints, Assumptions:
Goal:	Team Members:

Preliminary Project Plan	Target Date	Actual Date
Define		
Measure		
Analyze		
Improve		
Control		

Prepared by:		Approved by:	

Charter.

Helpful Note 1:

Phase 1 of Structure Analysis usually takes about four to eight hours to complete. There is a great tendency for first-time team members to lose focus and try to discuss possible solutions. Do not let them!

Some team members are uncomfortable with the narrow focused step-by-step approach to improvement. It is hard to see that the discipline of the specific phases leads to certain success. Stick with it.

Phase 2: Describe the current state or situation (Check/ Measure)

2.1 Investigate key features of the problem

2.1.1. Study the process. In this step the team members map the process or create workflow diagrams or flow charts to develop an understanding of the elements of the process. Inputs, outputs, measures, and owners (similar to the ISO systems approach). This helps identify the critical process components.

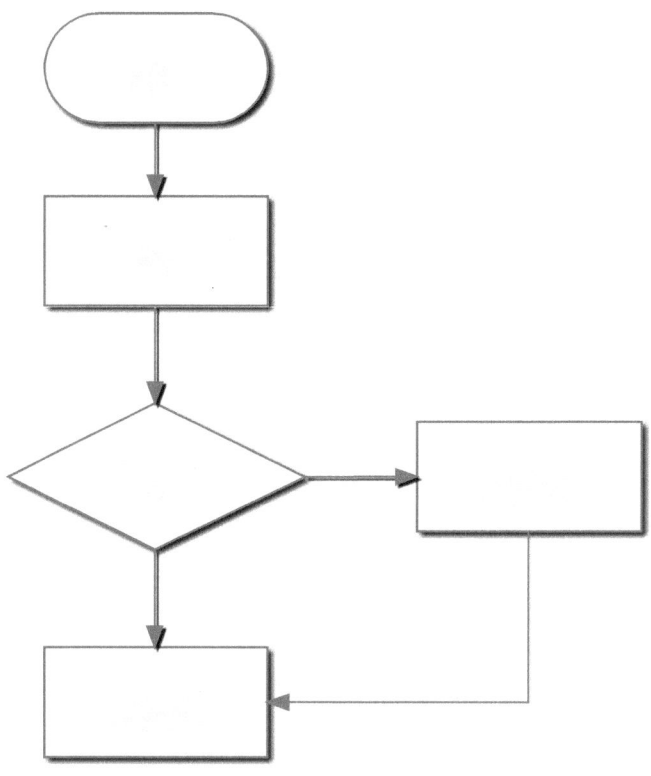

Flow Chart.

2.1.2. Develop theories that describe aspects of the problem.

This step narrows focus by developing theories that more specifically describe the problem. Common tools and methods are brainstorming, fishbone diagrams, or creating an is/is not matrix that identifies:

- o Who is affected by the problem,
- o What is happening when the problem occurs,
- o When the problem is occurring, and
- o Where the problem is occurring.

It is crucial to identify the size and scope of the issue.

Helpful Note 2:

When working with large systems (vs local processes), designing new systems, developing new products, or trying to understand complex systems, useful methods such as the 7 Management and Planning Tools work well. The tools are comprised of the Affinity chart, Interrelationship Digraph, Tree Diagram, and Process Decision Program Chart, and several others. They, in effect are the systems counterpart to a process flow chart. Other useful methods may be: Voice of the Customer, Quality Function Deployment, or Design Failure Mode and Effects Analysis.

2.1.3 Collect and chart data that support the theories. In this

step, data is collected and analyzed to support or refute

theories and hunches. The overall goal is to answer the question, "How do you know?" There may be hunches and theories for which no data exists. They may be legitimate potential root causes for problems or controlling factors for systems. They remain to be investigated.

Helpful Note 3:
If process data is available, it is often useful to create control charts of the process. A great deal of information may be derived such as process stability, statistical bounds, special causes of variation, or whether or not the system or process has changed over time.

2.2   Developing strategies and measures of progress

2.2.1   Determine Strategies. Determine how the theories will be investigated and assign task owners.

2.2.2   Determine Measures. This step will answer the question: If successful how will we know it? There may be multiple measures of progress or success.

2.2.3.   Set Improvement Targets.   Evaluating the problem involves acquiring data. The data will help determine improvement feasibility and the magnitude of improvement

Helpful Note 4:

Phase 2 of the Structured Analysis usually takes from two to several weeks to complete. The information collected in this step is critical to the success of the project. It will cull the list of theories so that detailed investigation can occur in Phase 3.

Phase 3: Analyzing Root Causes (Analyze)

3.1 Developing and prioritizing theories

3.1.1. Diagram cause-and-effect relationships. In this step the team constructs detailed cause-and-effect diagrams that explain the cause-and-effect relationships for the key features of the problems identified in Phase 2.

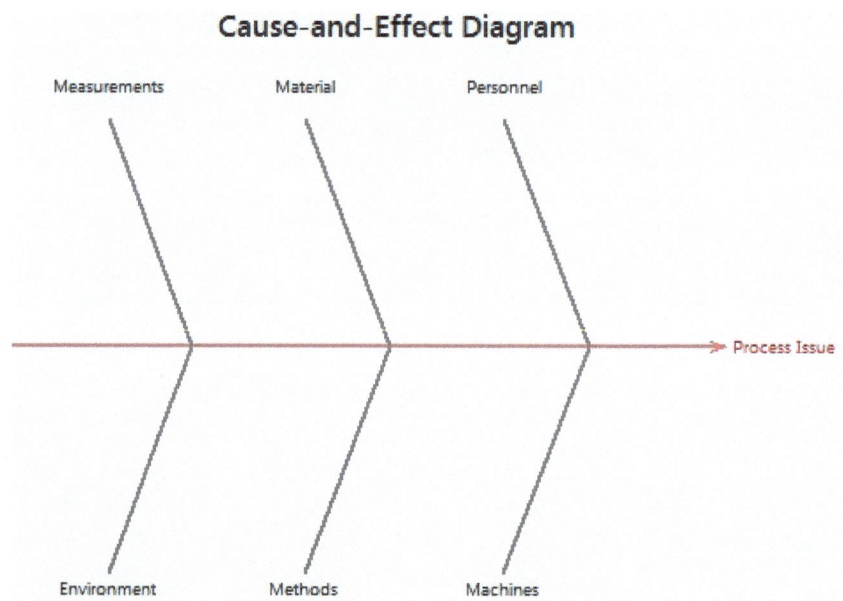

Cause and Effect Diagram.

Helpful Note 5:

In Minitab version 17, the Cause and Effect (Fishbone) Diagram includes: Personnel, Method, Measurements, Material,

Environment, and Machine. In Phase 3 a team may have a fishbone for each of these domains.

3.1.2 Refine diagram of causes. This step involves studying the potential causes or controlling factors by determining the data available to verify or eliminate potential factors. The objective is to narrow the list of causes. The end result is a simplified cause-and-effect diagram with a high probability of containing a controlling factor or root cause.

3.1.3 Prioritize theories for root causes. Team members answer the question: which causes are consistent with available data and what causes need additional study? With that information a prioritized for verifying theories.

3.2 Verifying theories with data

3.2.1. Collect information to verify root causes. Collect the data to verify or dismiss potential controlling factors or root causes. The data will answer the question, *how do we know* that the correct causes or controlling factors have been identified.

3.2.2. Integrate information collected. In this task, you compile and study the data as it's collected to identify the MAIN root cause or controlling factor. This will often require evidence of correlation between the cause and effect. Before and after process change comparison is important.

Helpful Note 6:

Regression analysis is a very useful statistical method. Correlation between controlling factors and response variables should have a high coefficient of determination value; a high R^2.

3.2.3. Reproduce problem to verify causes. If possible, intentionally reproduce the problem to verify that the correct root cause has been identified. With some processes, it is difficult or impossible to reproduce the problem; particularly when making adjustments to a live process. Take care to avoid creating additional problems for your customers.

Phases 1 through 3 of Structured Analysis usually take the longest to complete, but if the time is well-spent, the root causes or controlling factors will be known. If not done properly, the wrong, or no, conclusions may be drawn leading to insignificant or even counterproductive changes.

Phase 4: Developing improvements (Plan/Improve)

Most of the difficult work precedes Phase 4. This is because determining the controlling factors for processes often requires investigating what has been unknown and, sometimes, is more difficult than anticipated. If analysis has been successfully concluded, however, solutions present themselves. The development improvement phase can be one of the most satisfying.

Helpful Note 7:

Avoiding shooting from the hip.

4.1. Select the improvements to be made

4.1.1. Generate various alternatives. In this step, the team develops alternative solutions for improving or removing the most significant root cause(s) of the problem. A Decision Tree is often used to list the options. Items on the decision tree can be prioritized based on risk or importance.

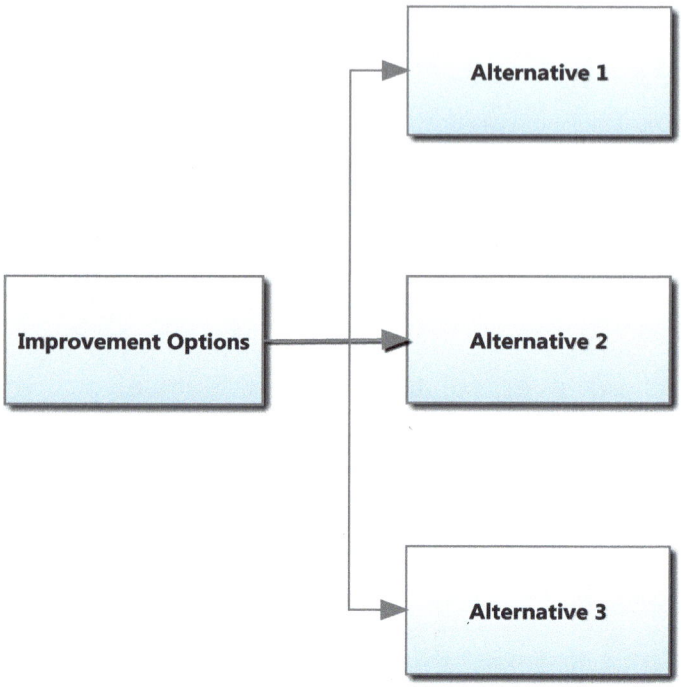

Decision Tree.

4.1.2. Determine the improvements to be made. In this step, each possible solution is evaluated using specific criteria established by the team. Then, select the improvements to be made ensuring that everyone involved understands the improvements.

4.2 Plan, schedule and budget the implementation. After selecting the improvements, it may be required to create a detailed plan for implementing the improvements, possibly even a timeline or a Gantt Chart. Again, it's important to make sure that all those affected are involved, and that the plan consists of information

18

on who, what, when, where, why, how, and how much for each implementation step.

Helpful Note 8:

By the time a team reaches Phase 4, they usually feel like they're finally accomplishing their theme (goal), so the pace of the project seems to pick up. It is a good time to prepare a Storyboard to display the project to the organization.

Phase 5: Verifying results (Do/Improve – Check Improvement)

In Phase 4 of the Structured Analysis, the team selected, planned, scheduled, and budgeted for the solutions or improvements. In completing Phase 4. The team also completed the "Plan" stage of the Plan-Do-Check-Act (PDCA) cycle. Phase 4 also corresponds to the Improve step in 6 Sigma's DMAIC.

Phase 5 corresponds with the "Do" and "Check" stages of the PDCA cycle. As was the Improve step in 6 Sigma. There are two steps within Phase 5.

5.1. Implementing and verifying on small scale

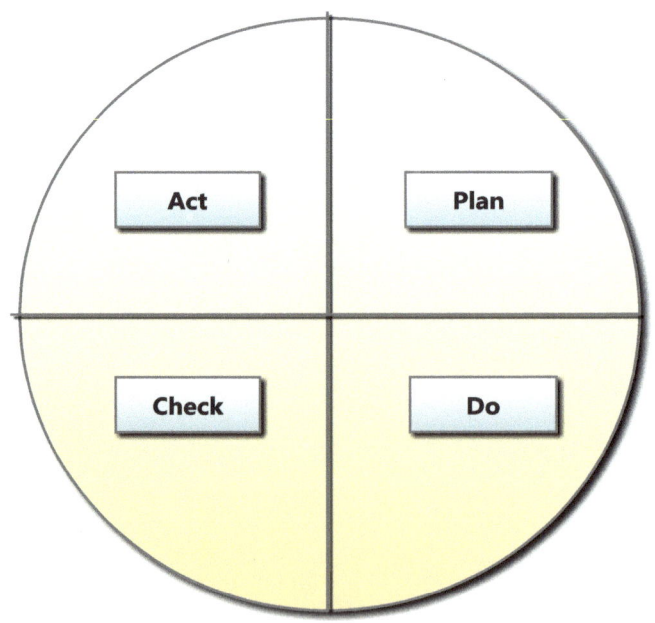

Shewhart's Cycle.

5.1.3. Upgrade the plan ("Act"). At this point, the team takes the information from Step 5.1.2 to determine if the plan needs to be revised. Often workers involved in the small-scale implementation have suggestions for improving the implementation. Or, sometimes the proposed improvements have negative effects in other parts of a process. This step tries to account for those eventualities.

5.2 Implementing and verifying on full scale

5.2.1. Implement the improvements on a full scale ("Do"). Finally, it's time to implement the proposed improvements throughout the entire system. It is, again, important to answer the five W's and two H's.

5.2.2. Verify the full-scale results ("Check"). At this stage, the team studies the results of the full-scale implementation to verify whether root causes and controlling factors have been positively affected. It is also important to estimate the benefits of the implementation. All involved need to know the measure of success.

Phase 6: Standardizing improvements (Act/Improve-Control)

In Phase 5 of Structured Analysis, the team implemented improvements on a small scale and checked those improvements to see whether they had the intended result. If the small scale improvements were successful, then full-scale implementation was deployed.

In the past, many or most projects ended at Phase 5. The concept of control was ignored. This resulted in potentially losing the gains in an improvement project.

6.1. Establishing control items, methods

6.1.1. Determine how to monitor critical quality characteristics.

Typically, the initial measure identified early in the project can also become the control item. Depending on the analysis, other measures may be determined. Typical control items may involve dimensions, quantity, time, percent, volumes, and so on.

This particular step of has several objectives. They are:
- o To identify the critical characteristics for the quality of the results of the process; product or service.
- o To determine which quality characteristics are indicators of the stability of the process.

- To determine the method for monitoring the results of the process, product or service.

6.1.2. Determine how to monitor critical process characteristics.

Having determined what to measure, it is now important to determine the 5 W's and 2 H's:

- Who will check the process?
- What part of the process will be checked?
- When will the process be checked?
- Where will the process be checked?
- Why will the process be checked?
- How will the process be checked?
- How often will the process be checked?

All of this information must be clearly documented in a Control Plan, one of the most important documents in quality assurance. In industry, it is often a binding contractual document and part of Advance Product Quality Planning, Product Realization, or Verification and Validation.

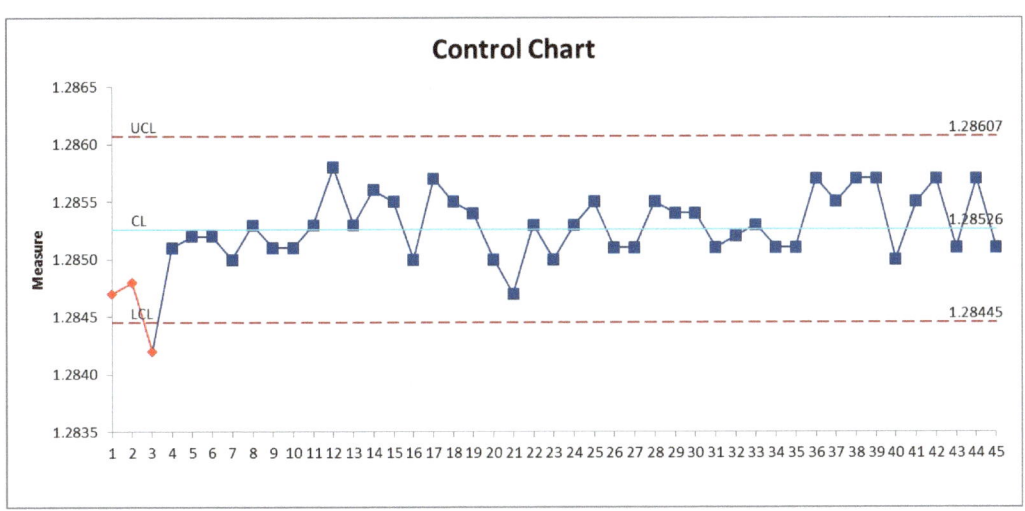

Individual and Moving Range Chart.

6.2 Standardization

6.2.1 Standardizing key items

In this step, the team finalizes a Control Plan. The standardized Control Plan should be communicated to all involved workers. That includes the critical daily work methods developed throughout the course of the project. Tracking and monitoring control charts may be a part of new standardized procedures.

Often in an organization, there are similar processes in different areas. Step 6.2 is where transferal may occur. They may be considered preventive actions.

	Prototype	Prelaunch	Production	Key Contact/Phone		Date(Orig)	Date (Rev.)
Control Plan Number							
Part Number/Latest Change Level				Core Team		Customer Eng. Approval/Date	
Part Name/Description				Organization/Plant Approval/Date		Customer Quality Approval/Date (If Req'd)	
Organization/Plant			Organization Code	Other Approval/Date (If Req'd)		Other Approval/Date (If Req'd)	

Part/ Process Number	Process Name/ Operation Description	Machine, Device, Jig, Tools, for Mfg.	Characteristics			Special Char. Class	Product/Process Specification/ Tolerance	Methods				Reaction Plan
			No.	Product	Process			Evaluation/ Measurement Technique	Sample		Control Method	
									Size	Freq		
x1	Check in Time							?????				Check time???

Manufacturing Control Plan.

Phase 7: Conclude the project (Check, Plan)

In Phase 6 of the process, the team standardized the process improvements, created Control Plans, and communicated all changes to the affected areas. This concludes the project and what remains is to review the Structure Analysis record and approve by signing off.

7.1 Review.

7. 1.1 Checking results, describing what was learned. The review includes team members verifying that the project's original objectives were met. If they were not met, the team may have to go back to step 2 and go through the improvement process again. The team may also want to go back and study the improvement process to determine what went well and what could have been improved.

The objectives to close the project are to:

- o Identify the gains by comparing the baseline measurement of the process (before improvement) to the measures of progress after improvement. Comparison of run charts, control charts, histograms, and any other charts from Phases 2 and 3 with evidence in Phase 5 will show a measurable degree of improvement.

- o Determine how much of each root cause was reduced or eliminated.
- o Decide whether to end the project or cycle through the improvement process again for further improvement.
- o Study what was learned about customers, suppliers, the work process, and the way Structured Analysis was completed (each step of the process, the charts used, the time spent on the different parts of the process, etc.).
- o Develop a list of other problems that you discovered during the improvement process.

7.2 Sign off and Closure.

Key management review, request edits, clarification, or modification and when satisfied, sign off on the projects.

Notes on Final Documentation and Potential Future Plans

After the project is completed, it can be useful to document the valuable information gathered during the project. Therefore, the three main objectives of this sub step are to:

1. Prepare for future projects by summarizing remaining problems, deciding which   problems should be addressed in future projects, and developing initial plans for improving these problems.

2. Document your improvement process in a "QC story" (Quality Control story).   This is a very short report (or storyboard) of the few charts and graphs that best summarize each step of the improvement process.

3. Close the project by celebrating your accomplishments, along with the people who helped make it possible (co-workers who helped do your work so you could attend team meetings, suppliers who changed their processes to make your improvements possible, and anyone else who contributed to your success).

Process improvement projects can take six months to over a year to complete, and it's important to recognize the commitment it takes to see a project through to the end.

4. It is helpful to track team progress with a tracking matrix such as the one below. If a project stalls, it will show up quickly as a horizontal line on the chart.

Tracking a Project.

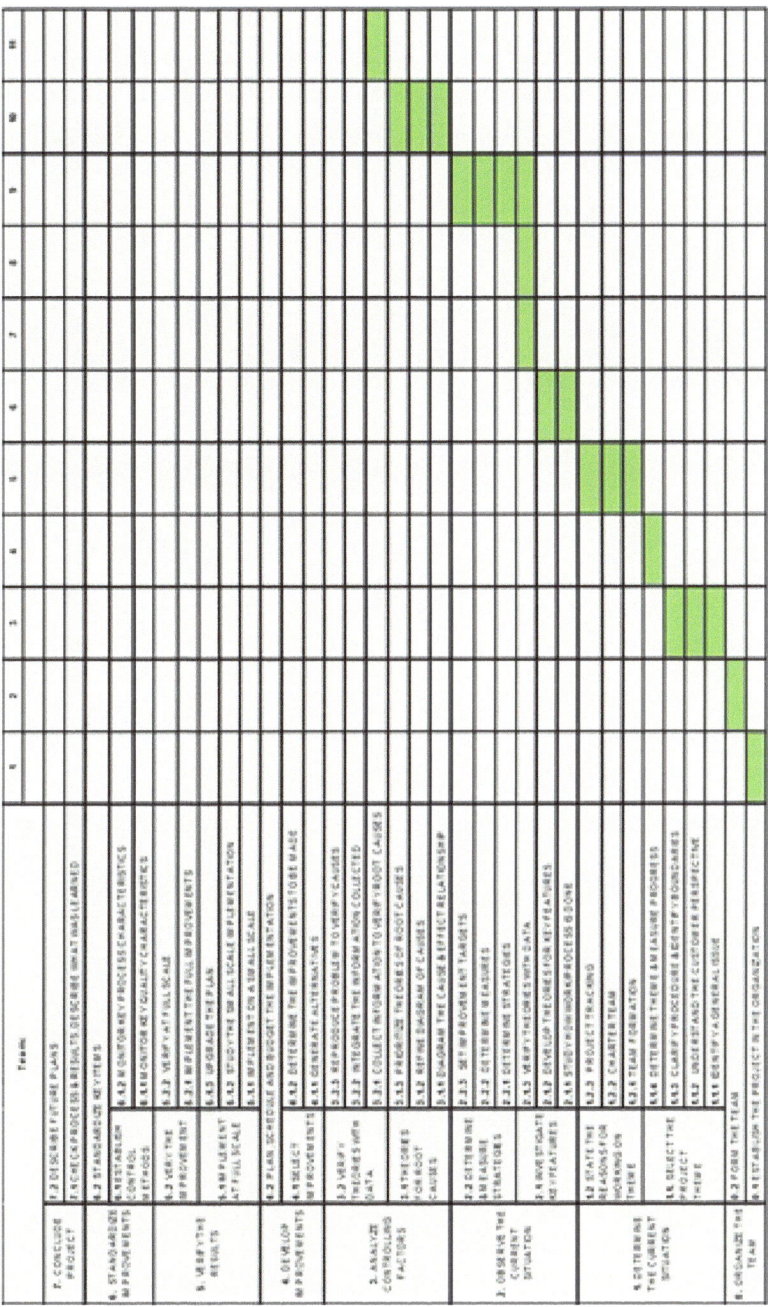

Project Tracking Using Excel

www.ingramcontent.com/pod-product-compliance
Lightning Source LLC
Chambersburg PA
CBHW050415180526
45159CB00005B/2287